Trees

Written by Sarah Betteridge
and Sarah Lyne

Collins

Trees are all around us.
See them in the street. See them
on the farm.

Step into the woods for a good look at trees.

spring

summer

In the spring trees get buds
and blooms. In the summer
trees are green.

4

winter

evergreen

As winter comes,
we can just see sticks
and twigs. Trees can
be evergreen too.

Conkers are seeds.

Trees come from seeds.
Seeds drop onto the ground.

The sun and rain feed the seeds.
The roots push into the soil.
Then the tree stems soon
shoot up.

Some animals can sleep in trees.
They can nest in the treetops.

Trees shelter us, too. They keep the rain off. Wood cabins are snug.

train set

bunk bed

blocks

Wood comes from trees.
Lots of things are wooden.

books

box

We get paper and card from wood pulp.

Trees can be lots of fun too!

We must all look after trees.

Seeds

Shelters

seed

wood

stem

14

Things from trees

bunk bed

blocks

paper

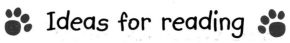 Ideas for reading

Written by Clare Dowdall, PhD
Lecturer and Primary Literacy Consultant

Learning objectives: *(reading objectives correspond with Red B band; all other objectives correspond with Purple band)* read simple words by sounding out and blending the phonemes all through the word from left to right; read a range of familiar and common words and simple sentences independently; give some reasons why things happen; explain organizational features of texts, including alphabetical order, layout, diagrams, captions, hyperlinks and bullet points; explain ideas and processes using imaginative and adventurous vocabulary and non-verbal gestures to support communication

Curriculum links: Science

Focus phonemes: ee, ou, sh, er, ar, oo (look), oo (bloom), th, oi

Fast words: are, all, come

Resources: magnetic letters, pencils, paper

Word count: 156

Getting started

- Look at the front cover together and read the title. Ask children to describe what they like about trees and how they think trees help us.

- Ask children to read the blurb aloud. Look at the words *trees* and *around.* For these words, ask children to practise sounding out each phoneme and blending them to read. Notice that the words have long vowel sounds made from two letters, e.g. *ee, ou.*

- Explain that this is an information book. Walk through the book looking for features of information books, e.g. labels and photographs.

Reading and responding

- Turn to pp2–3. Read the text with the children and ask them to describe what they can see when they look at a tree.

- Ask children to read pp4–5 quietly. Ask children to describe what is happening to the tree and discuss how trees change with the seasons.